The Science of Living Things

What is a
Reptile?

Bobbie Kalman

Crabtree Publishing Company

The Science of Living Things Series
A Bobbie Kalman Book

**For Jennifer Kala Kos
Power to the turtle!**

Author and Editor-in-Chief
Bobbie Kalman

Managing editor
Lynda Hale

Senior editor
April Fast

Research and editing team
Allison Larin
Kate Calder
Heather Levigne
Jane Lewis
Marsha Baddeley

Computer design
Lynda Hale

**Production coordinator
and photo researcher**
Hannelore Sotzek

Color separations and film
Dot 'n Line Image Inc.
CCS Princeton (cover)

Special thanks to
Dr. Christopher Brochu and Harold K. Voris, Field Museum
of Natural History; Jim Cornish, Gander Academy; Ryan T. Carter

Photographs
James Kamstra: pages 6 (bottom), 17 (middle), 22 (left)
Robert & Linda Mitchell: pages 11 (top), 17 (top), 19 (bottom),
    22 (right), 25 (bottom)
Photo Researchers, Inc./Andrew A. Gifford/NAS: page 12
James H. Robinson: pages 11 (bottom), 17 (bottom), 19 (top)
James P. Rowan: pages 6 (top), 13 (bottom), 24 (bottom), 26 (bottom left),
    27 (top), 29
Tony & Alba Sanches-Zinnanti: page 11 (middle)
Allen Blake Sheldon: pages 9 (bottom), 13 (top), 14, 16, 26 (top), 30
Eric A. Soder/Tom Stack & Associates: page 15
Valan Photos: John Cancalosi: pages 20 (bottom), 28; James D. Markou:
    page 27 (bottom); Jim Merli: page 20 (top); John Mitchell: page 21
Visuals Unlimited: page 13 (middle)
Other photographs by Digital Stock and Digital Vision

Illustrations
Barbara Bedell: cover, pages 4-5, 7; Anne Giffard: page 21

Printer
Worzalla Publishing Company

Crabtree Publishing Company

PMB 16A	612 Welland Avenue	73 Lime Walk
350 Fifth Avenue	St. Catharines	Headington
Suite 3308	Ontario, Canada	Oxford OX3 7AD
New York	L2M 5V6	United Kingdom

Cataloging in Publication Data
Kalman, Bobbie
    What is a reptile?

(The science of living things)
Includes index.

ISBN 0-86505-881-4 (library bound) ISBN 0-86505-893-8 (pbk.)
This book describes the main types of reptiles and their physiology, habitats,
behavior, diet, and offspring.

1. Reptiles—Juvenile literature. [1. Reptiles.] I. Title. II. Series: Kalman, Bobbie.
Science of living things.

QL644.2.K35 1999   j597.9   LC 98-37548
                                                               CIP

Contents

What is a reptile?

Reptiles are **vertebrate** animals. They have a **spine**, or backbone. Reptiles are **cold-blooded**, but their blood is not actually cold. Cold-blooded means that the temperature of their body changes with the temperature of their surroundings. All reptiles hatch from eggs. The body of a reptile is covered with protective **scales** or horny **plates**. Some reptiles have short legs. Others have no legs at all. Reptiles have lungs for breathing, just as you do.

Reptile groups
Scientists divide reptiles into four main groups:
1. lizards and snakes
2. chelonians
3. crocodilians
4. tuataras

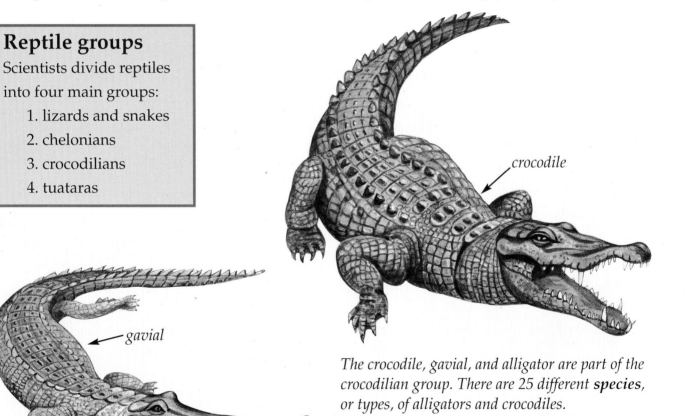

crocodile

gavial

*The crocodile, gavial, and alligator are part of the crocodilian group. There are 25 different **species**, or types, of alligators and crocodiles.*

alligator

The tuatara is in its own group.
It is the oldest species of reptile.

This snake-necked turtle
(above) and giant tortoise
(below) belong to a group
of reptiles called chelonians.
Chelonians include all reptiles
with shells.

Lizards and snakes make up
the largest and most varied
group of reptiles.

chameleon

milk snake

The Komodo dragon is the largest
of all the lizards.

Reptile bodies

Different types of reptiles share many similar features. They all have **organs** such as a stomach, heart, and lungs inside their body. All reptiles have scaly skin, too.

Most reptiles continue growing new teeth throughout their life. As the old, damaged teeth fall out, new teeth grow in to replace them. Turtles, however, do not have teeth. They have a hard beak for breaking apart their food.

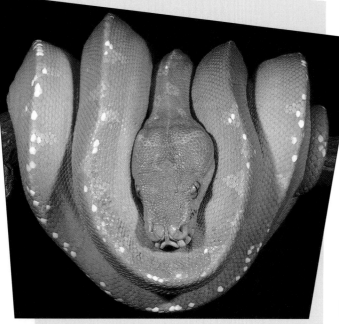

This green tree python rests by folding its long body over a tree branch.

Always growing

All snakes and some reptiles such as crocodiles and giant tortoises continue to grow even when they are adults. The longer a reptile lives, the larger it gets. Some tortoises can live to be over 100 years old! The giant tortoise in this photo is big, but it is also very gentle. How old do you think it is?

Scaly skin

A reptile's skin has hundreds of scales. Scales are made of **keratin**. Your fingernails and hair are also made of this material. Scales can be large or small, depending on the type and size of the reptile. Some scales grow bigger and stronger as the animal continues to grow.

Scales help protect a reptile's body. They allow reptiles to live in a dry climate without **dehydrating**, or losing too much water from their body. Living things need water to stay alive.

Off with the old...

The scales of snakes and lizards are continually replaced. As they get bigger, their scales **molt**, or shed. New skin and scales grow in place of the molted skin.

Lizards molt by losing big flakes of skin over a couple of days. Snakes molt their entire skin at once and slither out of it. The old skin is dry, whereas the new skin is soft and shiny.

A delicate balance

All reptiles are cold-blooded. Their body temperature depends on the temperature of their surroundings. Reptiles need heat from the sun to warm their body. They bask in the sun during the day. When the temperature rises too high, they cool down in the shade. Most reptiles live in warm places. They could not survive in high mountain areas or in the Arctic where the air can be freezing.

Hibernation

Tortoises and terrapins that live in a **temperate** climate **hibernate** through the cold winter. During hibernation, an animal hides and rests for a long period of time without eating or moving very much. It lives off the fat stored in its body. When the weather is warm again, the animal comes out of hibernation.

Small land tortoises hibernate by burying themselves in deep mud so the winter frost will not reach them. Some terrapins hibernate in the muddy bottom of lakes or rivers. Other reptiles hide during the hot summer months. Summer hibernation is called **estivation**. Reptiles that live in hot deserts estivate.

This crocodile is too large to cool off under a rock. Instead, it opens its mouth to let moisture evaporate from its body. It also rests in the shade, away from the sun's hot rays.

Not too hot and not too cold

A reptile's body temperature needs to be warm so that its organs can work properly. When its body temperature falls below 86-95°F (30-35°C), a reptile's heartbeat and breathing slow down, and its digestive system does not work well.

If a reptile eats a large meal when it is cold outside, its body temperature could drop too low for its body to digest the food properly. A reptile that cannot digest its food may die.

The leopard tortoise (above) and the western hognose snake (below) can survive in very hot temperatures because they have underground homes in which they can keep themselves cool.

Senses

A reptile relies on its senses to find food and locate objects. The senses a reptile uses most depend on its body type and **habitat**, or home. Some reptiles have excellent sight, whereas others sense the heat or vibrations around them.

Jacobson's organ

Many reptiles have an organ called **Jacobson's organ** on the roof of their mouth. It is used for taste and smell. Snakes and lizards use it to find food. They flick their tongue quickly in and out of their mouth. As they stick out their tongue, these reptiles catch scent particles from the air. By touching their tongue to their Jacobson's organ, they can determine if they are close to food. They can also sense nearby **prey** or enemies.

This blue-tongued lizard uses its tongue to taste and smell the air.

Reptile eyelids

Snakes and some lizards do not have eyelids like ours. Instead, they have clear eyelids that always cover their eyes for protection. Crocodilians also have extra eyelids that are clear. They help these reptiles see when they are under water.

This gecko's eyelid is so clear that it seems invisible. The entire eye is covered by the lid, so dirt stays out of the gecko's eyeball.

Sounds good to me

Most reptiles have an ear opening where sound enters and travels inside their head to the inner ear. Snakes do not have an ear opening, but they can detect noises. Sound travels through their skull into their inner ear. Some snakes do not rely on sound at all. They are so sensitive to temperature changes that they can feel heat coming from the body of a warm-blooded animal.

The lizard above has an ear opening through which sound enters its ear. Snakes such as the copperhead pit viper on the left do not have such an opening. They have special organs called "pits" between their eyes and nostrils. These pits can detect a rise or drop in temperature. When a warm-blooded animal passes by, a pit viper can strike it, even in the dark!

Food and hunting

Snakes can eat animals that are much larger than they are. A snake can take several hours to swallow a large animal and weeks to digest it. After such a big meal, a snake may not need to eat again for up to a year!

In order to survive, reptiles need to eat food. Many are **carnivores**. Carnivores are animals that eat meat. Some reptiles even eat other reptiles! Most chelonians and some lizards are **omnivores**. They eat both plants and meat.

Finding food

Reptiles have many ways of catching and eating food. Some carnivorous reptiles hunt their food. They use their senses to track down prey. Other reptiles such as crocodiles and alligators often let their prey come to them. They hide quietly until an animal wanders by and then snatch it with their powerful jaws. Each reptile on this page has a different way of getting its food.

The alligator snapping turtle, shown above, lures prey into its mouth using its tongue, which looks like a small worm! When a curious fish comes close to investigate, the turtle snaps its mouth shut and captures the fish.

The California king snake, shown below, kills an animal by squeezing it to death. It wraps its body around its prey and slowly squeezes tighter and tighter. Eventually, the animal dies because it cannot breathe.

The Komodo dragon, shown above, hunts and kills live animals for food. It eats eggs, which it steals from the nests of other animals. The Komodo dragon also eats dead animals. Eating dead animal flesh gives Komodo dragons really bad breath!

Reptile homes

Reptiles live all over the world, except in places that have very cold weather. More reptiles live in **tropical** areas than in areas that have a cold winter. Reptiles can live on land, in water, in trees, or underground.

Happy together

Many reptiles live in a **community**, or group. Some species of reptiles live with other species of reptiles. Some, such as tuataras, live with other animals.

Feet tell the tale

A reptile's body is well suited to its environment. If you look at a reptile's feet, you can tell where it lives. Reptiles that live in water have webs between their toes to help them swim. Lizards that climb trees have long toes to grip bark and branches. Burrowing lizards live underground and have sharp claws for digging. Reptiles that live in the desert have long scales sticking out from their toes to help them walk on sand.

Tree reptiles

Tree-dwelling reptiles have different ways of moving around. The flying snake lives in tall trees. To get from one branch to another, it leaps, flattens its body, and glides through the air. Lizards that live in trees often have a long tail for balancing and holding onto branches.

This furry capybara, shown above, shares its home with a group of dangerous-looking caimans. Fortunately, caimans eat only fish.

Baby reptiles

A male and a female reptile **mate** to produce more reptiles. Most species of reptiles lay eggs from which the babies hatch. Some reptiles such as boa constrictors keep the eggs inside their body, and the babies are born live.

Reptile eggs

Some female reptiles lay their eggs on land in a nest made of plants or mud. Some reptile eggs have hard shells like those of chicken eggs. Others have softer, leathery shells. Baby reptiles break through their shell using an **egg tooth**. The egg tooth dries up and falls off soon after the baby hatches. Many reptile eggs are eaten by **predators** before they hatch. Mammals, other reptiles, and raptors prey on reptile eggs.

These agamid lizard hatchlings are able to defend themselves and find food on their own.

Hatchlings

Young reptiles that have just hatched are called **hatchlings**. They look like small adult reptiles. Most hatchlings are able to care for themselves right away, so their mother does not need to look after them. Even after they are born, the hatchlings are still in danger of being eaten by predators.

What type of reptile do you think is growing inside these eggs? Look at the picture on the opposite page for a clue!

The best mom

Of all the reptiles, crocodilians spend the most time caring for their young. A female crocodilian will guard her nest from predators. Once her babies have hatched, she carries them to the water in her mouth. For several months, the hatchlings stay close to their mother for protection.

Self-defense

Reptiles have many ways of protecting themselves against their enemies. Some, like the Komodo dragon, use brute force to injure their attackers. Other reptiles have different ways of defending themselves.

Poisonous reptiles

Some snakes and lizards use **venom**, or poison, to protect themselves. Poisonous snakes and lizards have two extra teeth called **fangs** in their mouth. Fangs collapse against the roof of the reptile's mouth when they are not being used. When the reptile needs them, the fangs flip down and are ready to be used.

Some lizards try to scare off enemies by making themselves look threatening. This frilled lizard raises the ruff around its neck as it chases away an enemy.

Injecting venom

Fangs are hollow and very sharp. They work like a doctor's needle. The poison is produced in the reptile's venom sac. It travels through the hollow fangs into the hole that the fangs have made in the other animal. The poison in some reptiles can kill an enemy, whereas the poison in others merely stuns the enemy long enough to allow the reptile to get away.

People sometimes "milk" the venom out of poisonous snakes and collect it to use in medicines. To milk a snake, a person holds it by the head and gently squeezes venom from the venom sac inside. The venom then drips out of the snake's fangs.

Tails off to you!

Most lizards can drop their tail if a predator grabs it. A lizard's tail is made up of several bones called **vertebrae**. These vertebrae have cracks where they can break off. When the lizard drops its tail, the tail wiggles for a few minutes. This movement distracts the predator long enough for the lizard to escape. When the tail grows back, it does not have vertebrae. The new portion of the tail is a hollow tube of **cartilage**, or tough, flexible tissue. If the tail breaks off again, it must separate above the first break where there are still vertebrae.

This lizard's tail has dropped off. The new tail that grows in its place will be smaller than the original tail.

Snakes

The coral cobra, shown above, is poisonous. It uses poison to defend itself and stun or kill prey.

Snakes are long reptiles with no legs. Some live in underground tunnels, or **burrows**, and others live above ground. Snakes also live in water and in trees. The largest snakes in the world are the anaconda and the reticulated python. Each grows up to 30 feet (9 m) long. These snakes **constrict** their prey. Worm snakes, such as the Brahminy blind snake, are less than 6 inches (15 cm) long.

This rainbow boa constrictor kills its prey by squeezing it until it cannot breathe.

Eating

A snake's teeth are not for chewing. They are used for grabbing prey and pulling it down the snake's **gullet**, or throat. Snakes swallow their prey whole. Their gullet makes up one-third of their body length.

Poisonous snakes

Some people think all snakes are poisonous, but of the 2,700 species of snakes only 800 are venomous. Of those species, only 250 are dangerous to people. Most snakes bite only if they need to protect themselves.

*Hinges on a snake's jaws allow its mouth to open very wide. Some snakes can **dislocate**, or separate, their jaws to swallow very large prey.*

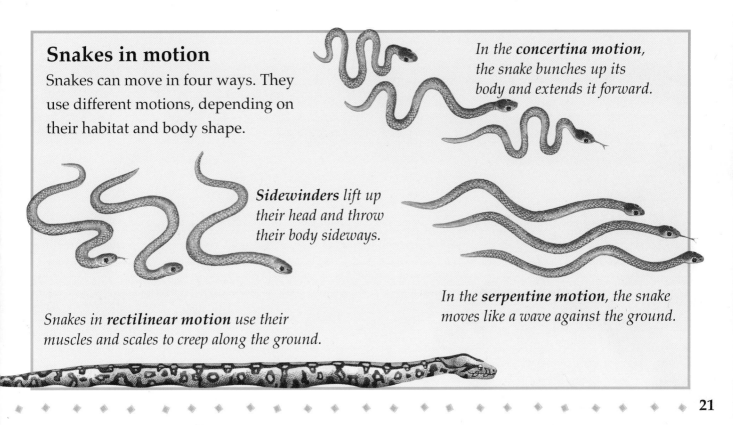

Snakes in motion

Snakes can move in four ways. They use different motions, depending on their habitat and body shape.

*In the **concertina motion**, the snake bunches up its body and extends it forward.*

***Sidewinders** lift up their head and throw their body sideways.*

*In the **serpentine motion**, the snake moves like a wave against the ground.*

*Snakes in **rectilinear motion** use their muscles and scales to creep along the ground.*

Lizards

Lizards are reptiles that have a tail and live mostly on land. Most lizards have four short legs, but a few species have no legs at all. Most lizards can run or move quickly. The males of some species are a different color than the females so they can attract a mate.

Little lizards, large lizards

Lizards come in all shapes and sizes. The prickly gecko, shown top left, is one of the smallest lizards in the world. The largest is the Komodo dragon, which can grow to 10 feet (3 m) long and weighs as much as 365 pounds (166 kg).

Monitor lizards

The largest lizards in the world, such as the Komodo dragon above, belong to the **monitor lizard** group. Monitor lizards have excellent vision and a strong sense of smell. They can unhinge their jaws and swallow prey whole. They are unpredictable and aggressive.

Chameleons

Chameleons are unique lizards. They can change the color of their skin to shades of green, yellow, brown, and red to blend in with their surroundings. Their ability to change color helps them hide from predators and sneak up on prey.

Eyes everywhere

A chameleon has bulging eyes that can swivel in different directions. One eye can be looking straight ahead while the other looks up. With swivel eyes, a chameleon can catch insects and watch for predators at the same time.

Getting around

A lizard's legs are on the sides of its body. The lizard has to bend its body from side to side in order to walk and run. Using this movement, it can move quickly.

Some lizards such as chameleons have a **prehensile** tail that helps support their body weight. When they are in trees, they often wrap their strong tail around branches to avoid falling. Some lizards such as the basilisk are able to run on their two hind legs.

This chameleon, shown above, is starting to change color to blend in with its rocky environment.

Chelonians

The sea turtle has legs like flippers to push it through the water quickly.

A chelonian is a reptile with a shell. Turtles and tortoises are chelonians. They make up the oldest living group of reptiles and include over 200 species. Chelonians are generally slow, but they are very strong and well protected by their shell. Turtles have good eyesight, but scientists believe that these reptiles use their sense of smell to find food and other members of their group.

Similar but different

Turtles and tortoises look similar, but they have some important differences. Turtles live in water, and tortoises live on land. Tortoises have thick, strong shells that protect them from predators. Turtles have thin, light shells that help them swim easily through the water.

The Galapagos tortoise has legs like an elephant's—short, strong, and sturdy to carry its heavy shell across land.

The important shell

Almost all turtles and tortoises have a tough shell that provides them with **camouflage** and protection. It is made up of plates of bone connected at the ribs and backbone. A thin layer of skin that contains many nerves and blood vessels covers the shell. This skin is covered with **scutes**, or horny plates, and makes the turtle very sensitive to touch. Chelonians do not molt their shells. The shells get thicker and larger as the animal gets older.

Its hard shell protects this small tortoise from predators. The scutes on a chelonian's shell fit together like the scales on a snake's body.

Soft-shelled turtles

The soft-shelled turtle in this picture has a different type of shell than that of other turtles. The shell is made up of thick skin, but it can be easily cut or damaged. Soft-shelled turtles live only in freshwater habitats. When they swim, they stick their snorkel-like snout out of the water so they can breathe. Many people keep soft-shelled turtles as pets.

Crocodilians

Most of the gavial population lives in India, Nepal, and Pakistan. These reptiles have a long, slender snout suited to catching fish.

There are three types of crocodilians—crocodiles, alligators, and gavials. Crocodilians are animals with sharp teeth, a long snout, a heavy body, and a large, muscular tail for swimming. Their skin is covered in horny plates or large scales. Crocodilians eat birds and fish. They are **nocturnal** predators that hunt for food at night. During the day, they bask in the sun.

Crocodile or alligator?

Look at these two pictures. Can you tell which is the crocodile and which is the alligator? Look at the snout of each one. The caiman, above left, is a member of the alligator family. It has a short, U-shaped snout that is ideal for crushing animals.

When its mouth is closed, only a few teeth show. The crocodile, above right, has a long, pointed, V-shaped snout. This type of snout helps the crocodile tear chunks of meat off its prey. Two large teeth on a crocodile's lower jaw show when its mouth is closed.

Crocodilian homes

All crocodilians live in shallow water, swamps, or slow-moving rivers. They live only in warm areas of the world, where the winters are rarely cold. Many crocodilians live together in large groups.

(right) These crocodiles live in the Nile river in Egypt. They live together in a small group. During mating season, the males fight with one another to mate with the female crocodiles.

*A crocodilian's eyes, nostrils, and ear openings are set high on its head, allowing it to breathe and see, even when most of its body is under water. **Membranes**, or thin layers of skin, close the nostrils, throat, and ears so water cannot get in when the animal dives.*

Tuataras

Although the tuatara looks like a lizard, it belongs to its own group. It is the only surviving species of a group of reptiles that lived 200 million years ago. Tuataras were on the earth long before other reptiles and even before dinosaurs. They are often called **living fossils** because they are living examples of creatures that were alive millions of years ago.

Sloooow motion

Tuataras have a slower **metabolism** than that of other reptiles. They digest their food and grow very slowly. Some tuataras, however, can grow to be over 2 feet (60 cm) long and live up to 120 years of age.

Where do tuataras live?

For many years tuataras lived in New Zealand and on the surrounding islands. Scientists believe that tuataras were able to survive for millions of years because there were no animals in New Zealand that killed or ate these slow-moving reptiles.

Tuataras changed very little over time because the conditions on the island on which they lived did not change. When people settled in New Zealand, however, they brought with them animals such as dogs and rats that killed these reptiles. Soon there were no more tuataras living in New Zealand. The islands off the coast of New Zealand are the only places in the world where tuataras now live.

Cold creatures

Tuataras are more active in colder temperatures than other reptiles. They hunt and eat at night when the air is cool. Tuataras feed on insects, small animals, and bird's eggs. During warm days, they sleep underground in burrows where some seabirds also live.

Tuataras are scaly and have a tail and face like a lizard's. They have a crest of small spines running down their back, and their teeth are the jagged edges of their jawbones that poke through their gums.

Dangers to reptiles

Like all animals, reptiles are an important part of the **food chain**. A food chain is a pattern, or cycle, of eating and being eaten. Reptiles eat insects and other animals for energy. As part of the cycle, some other animals get their energy by eating reptiles.

Pest controllers

People need reptiles. Some areas in the world have too many insects that eat people's crops. Many lizards eat insects. They help humans by controlling populations of insects that are considered to be pests.

The corn snake above is eating a mouse. Snakes help control the population of mice and rats.

Reptile predators

Reptiles are eaten by mammals such as mongooses, cats, and pigs. Birds of prey such as owls, eagles, and hawks eat reptiles as well. Other reptiles such as Nile crocodiles, king snakes, and monitor lizards also eat small reptiles. King cobras eat mainly snakes, which are smaller than they are. They even eat snakes of their own species!

The greatest threat

Reptile populations around the world are threatened by the destruction of their natural habitats. Habitats are destroyed when humans pollute the water and clear trees from the rainforests. Reptiles often die when their homes are destroyed. Snakes are disappearing faster than any other group of vertebrates.

Dinosaur cousins

Reptiles have been on the earth for about 340 million years—much longer than humans and other mammals. Dinosaurs belonged to the reptile family. The reptiles of today are relatives of the dinosaurs. Crocodiles are the closest living relatives of dinosaurs.

*Dinosaurs lived on the earth millions of years ago. They became **extinct**, or died off, long before humans lived on the earth. It is too late to save the dinosaurs, but people can take greater care to keep other reptiles alive.*

Glossary

burrow A tunnel or hole dug by an animal

camouflage The ability to blend in with natural surroundings

cold-blooded Describing an animal whose body temperature changes with the temperature of its environment

constrict To squeeze tightly

egg tooth A small tooth used to break out of a shell

environment Surroundings of a living thing

estivate To be in an inactive state during the summer

hibernate To be in an inactive state during the winter

mate To reproduce, or make babies

metabolism The system that the body uses to convert food into energy

nocturnal Describing an animal that sleeps during the day and hunts and eats at night

plates Thick, hard scales

predators Animals that hunt other animals

prehensile tail Describing a tail that can wrap around objects

prey Animals that are hunted and eaten by other animals

scales Thin sections of tissue that make up the skin of some reptiles

temperate Describing climate that is neither too hot nor too cold

tropical Describing hot, wet climate

vertebrate An animal with a backbone

warm-blooded Describing an animal whose body temperature stays the same regardless of the temperature of its environment

Index

2 3 4 5 6 7 8 9 0 Printed in the U.S.A. 7 6 5 4 3 2 1 0